IMAGES OF ENGLAND

HANDSWORTH
VOLUME II

MERRY X'MAS.

HAPPY NEW YEAR

LIEUT. LEMPRIER
AERONAUT
BIRMINGHAM

IMAGES OF ENGLAND

HANDSWORTH
VOLUME II

MARIA TWIST

TEMPUS

Frontispiece: Lieutenant George Lemprière (1856-1949) in the early twentieth century. Lieutenant Lemprière of Handsworth was famous as a balloonist and parachutist. He gave demonstrations at fêtes and outdoor events throughout Britain and Europe. This design was produced as a Christmas greetings card.

First published 2004

Tempus Publishing Limited
The Mill, Brimscombe Port,
Stroud, Gloucestershire, GL5 2QG
www.tempus-publishing.com

British Library Cataloguing in Publication Data.
A catalogue record for this book is available from the British Library.

ISBN 0 7524 3358 X

Typesetting and origination by Tempus Publishing Limited.
Printed in Great Britain.

Contents

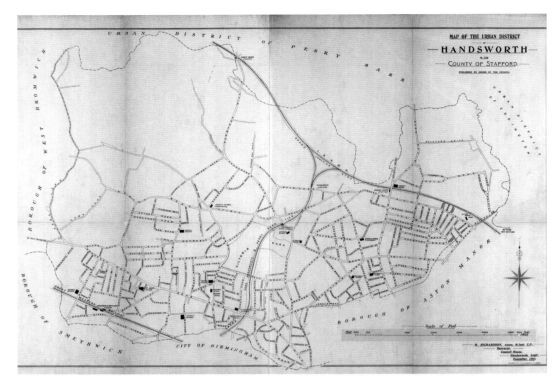

A map of the urban district of Handsworth in 1903. Handsworth was governed by a local board of health until the urban district was formed under the provisions of the Local Government Act of 1894. In 1911, Handsworth became part of the City of Birmingham.

Acknowledgements

Most of the photographs in this book are from Birmingham Central Library's own collection and I should like to thank Brian Gambles for his permission to use these. I also thank Mrs P. Burkill of the Handsworth Historical Society for permission to use the following photographs: p.20 bottom, p.35 top and bottom, p.36 top, p.37 bottom, p.40 top, p.49 bottom, p.50 bottom, p.52, p.59 bottom, p.60 top, p.81 bottom, p.84 top and p.102 top. I should like to thank Mr R. Shephard, the head teacher of Handsworth Grammar School, for permission to use the two photographs on p.78 which have been deposited in the Birmingham City Archives. The *Birmingham Post and Mail* Ltd have allowed me to use the following photographs: p.96 top, p.110 bottom, p.113, p.115 top and p.117 bottom. The photographs on p.2 and p.124 are from the Lemprière Collection in Birmingham City Archives. Attempts to trace the current copyright holders have been unsuccessful.

My thanks are also owed to Richard Albutt of the Handsworth Digital Project, without whose help I could not have coped with the technical problems, and to ex-colleagues in the Local Studies and History Service of Birmingham Central Library, particularly Paul Taylor and Andrew Willis. Last but not least, my husband Frank Twist has given me his unfailing support for which I am very grateful.

Introduction

In compiling this second selection of Handsworth photographs, my aim has been to choose those which would best complement the first volume from the rich collection of archival images available to me. This book covers a period of more than a hundred years, from the 1870s to the 1980s, during which time, Handsworth saw many changes.

Handsworth is a large, sprawling suburb to the north-west of Birmingham city centre and was part of the county of Staffordshire until it was absorbed by Birmingham in 1911. I have covered the old parish of Handsworth, including Handsworth Wood but excluding Perry Barr. I am aware that I have strayed across the boundary in some instances; I hope my artistic licence will be forgiven! Handsworth borders both inner city areas and leafy suburbs and has a great deal of variety and contrast. I hope I have reflected this in my selection of photographs.

Handsworth's heyday was perhaps the eighteenth century when it was renowned for the Soho Manufactory and the partnership between Matthew Boulton and James Watt. In spite of this, it never became highly industrialised but developed into a pleasant residential suburb with few back-to-back houses and many streets of good-quality terraced housing. There were also many larger houses belonging to wealthy manufacturers from Boulton and Watt onwards. Sadly, very few of these remain, although there are many fine nineteenth- and early twentieth-century houses. From the 1930s, more modest housing estates such as the Cherry Orchard Estate and the Hamstead Hall Estate were built on land which had been farm land.

Handsworth's greatest amenity is its beautiful park which was first laid out in 1888 and was added to subsequently. Local people enjoyed many local events held in the park, including the Birmingham Show, the Scouts' rally, and the Arena Theatre's 'Plays in the Park'. In April 2004, it was announced that the park would receive a magnificent grant of £8.4 million to restore and improve its facilities, including restoring and extending the Sons of Rest pavilion.

There were many features of life in Handsworth in the 1940s and 1950s which were shared by other city suburbs but may be worth describing for the benefit of younger readers. The winter of 1947 was particularly severe as Handsworth suffered blizzards which seemed to last for days and resulted in snow drifts piled up against the front door. The water pipes in some houses were frozen and people without water had to fetch water from houses where the pipes were not frozen, in our case from our next-door neighbour.

In the immediate post-war period, the milkman and baker still used horses for their deliveries and lucky children were allowed to ride on the milk float next to the milkman. On May Day, the horses would be gaily decorated. Many foods were still rationed and there were often long queues for fish or other scarce items. Clothing coupons had to be saved up to buy new clothes so children usually had clothes made out of adults' old dresses or coats and hardly knew what it was to have completely new garments. I vividly remember the excitement when sweets came off ration a few years after the war and children descended on the local post office to spend their pocket money. On the corner of the road opposite our house was a pig bin for kitchen waste which often contained half or even whole loaves of bread, presumably too stale for all but the pigs.

Everyone had coal fires in those days and the arrival of the chimney sweep was another excitement. Children would rush outside to see if the sweep's brush was emerging from the chimney pot. It was rumoured that some people would deliberately set fire to their chimney to avoid having to pay for the chimney sweep! Sometimes an exotically dressed gipsy woman would appear as if from nowhere selling the old type of wooden pegs and offering to tell your fortune if you crossed her palm with silver. We also used to see 'French onion men' as we called them; these came from Brittany with their bicycles festooned with strings of onions to sell. They invariably wore black berets so we knew they were real French men!

One of the highlights of the 1950s was the coronation in 1953. We listened to the ceremony on the radio as we didn't have a television. Some people bought televisions especially for the occasion but they were comparatively expensive and often only had 9in screens. Afterwards, we saw a film version of the coronation at our local cinema. It was in colour and was much better than the black and white television available then. At school, we practised for weeks for the coronation concert held in the playground. We sang songs from England, Scotland, Wales and Ireland and danced country dances such as Strip the Willow and the Gay Gordons. After more than fifty years, I can still feel the euphoria of that time.

There were no coal mines within the Birmingham boundary, but two lay just beyond it. Hamstead Colliery was still working when I was young and I remember being fascinated by the sight of the overhead trucks dropping their load of coal on to the pit heaps. I think Sandwell Park Colliery had already ceased working but the area still retained its coating of coal dust; a rather sinister-looking pool next to the colliery called Warstone or Wasson Pool was completely black. It is now called Swan Pool and looks far more attractive than it once did.

From the 1950s onwards, Handsworth saw immigration from the West Indies and later from the Indian sub-continent. This has brought events such as the Handsworth carnival, second only to the Notting Hill carnival in size. It is a lively and very colourful addition to the culture of the area. It has also brought social problems linked to unemployment and poor housing, which led to the notorious riots of 1985. Although problems remain, we must hope that everyone will be able to live in harmony and keep Handsworth a good place in which to live.

To readers who have internet access I would recommend the Handsworth Digital Project website, which has further information, photographs and maps of Handsworth. The address is: www.digitalhandsworth.org.uk.

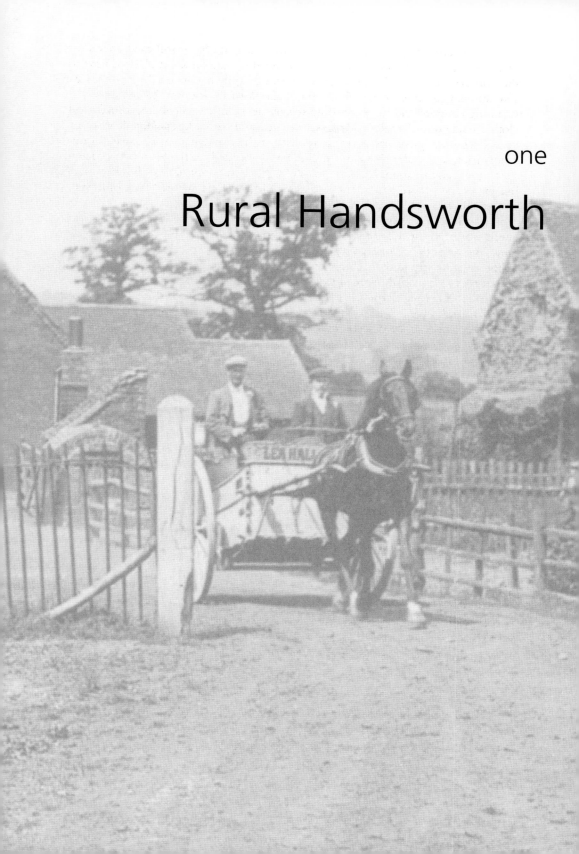

one

Rural Handsworth

Crick Farm pre-1904. The farmhouse was built in about 1709 and was named after the Crick, a way from Soho Road to Hamstead Road which had probably been a footpath to the old parish church of St Mary. The name survives in the present day Crick Lane.

These old cottages, photographed in Laurel Road in November 1896, were known as jaw-bone cottages because they had the jaw-bone of a whale on each side of the entrance gates. Laurel Road off Oxhill Road used to be referred to as 'Jaw-bones Lane' for this reason.

Cottages in Holyhead Road near Camp Lane, *c.* 1900.

A group of cottages near Nineveh Road, *c.* 1900. Records show that in 1829, a bull-bait took place here near Queen's Head Road. This was a late instance of this activity. Spectators would allegedly watch the bull-baiting from the branches of several tall trees which stood in the vicinity.

Right: A cottage in Hamstead Road opposite the end of Hall Road, *c.* 1900.

Below: Old cottages at the corner of Camp Lane and Holyhead Road in 1906.

A farm in Sandwell Lane in 1906. This may be Hermitage Farm, also known as Williamson's Farm, which existed until the 1920s. Sandwell Lane is now known as Sandwell Road.

Camp Lane in the snow, *c.* 1900. On the left is one of the lodges to the Leveretts, a large house on the site of Handsworth cemetery.

Island Lane, now Island Road, off Sandwell Road in 1906. A fine gas lamp stands at the road junction.

Sandwell Road, nearly opposite Island Road, in 1906. Handsworth kept its rural character well into the twentieth century as this photograph demonstrates.

Sandwell Road from the top of the hill in 1905. The lady on the left is pushing a bicycle; perhaps it is a Sunday afternoon. Long skirts would have made cycling rather a hazardous activity!

Island Road looking towards Sandwell Road in 1905.

Right: A view of the site of Handsworth cemetery in 1908.

Below: The corner of Oxhill Road and Camp Lane at the site of Handsworth's cemetery in 1908.

Above and below: The site of Handsworth cemetery in 1908.

An old farm in Holyhead Road opposite Island Road in 1906.

A house and its barns in Hamstead Hill in October 1897. The picture shows the corner of Somerset Road and Hamstead Hill.

A close-up of the house and barns shown in the previous photograph in 1896.

A rear view of the house and barns in Hamstead Hill in October 1896.

Above: Lea Hall Farm in Wood Lane, *c.* 1900. Known as the pink cottage, this was regarded as the oldest cottage in Handsworth.

Right: The farmer at Lea Hall Farm, *c.* 1900.

Opposite above: Another view of the barns in the process of demolition in October 1896.

Opposite below: Calthorpe cottages in Wood Lane on 22 May 1968. These are mid-eighteenth-century estate cottages, probably of seventeenth-century origin. They have now been refurbished and converted into four cottages.

Lea Hall Farm, *c.* 1900.

The farmer's wife at Lea Hall Farm,
c. 1900.

Cherry Orchard Farm in June 1896. The pool is called Arm's Pool after the farmer, Charlie Arm.

Cherry Orchard Farm pre-1930. Cherry Orchard Farm was one of the larger farms in Handsworth and was said to date from the fourteenth century. The farm house, which was there until 1930, was certainly built much more recently but could have replaced an earlier house. The farm was sold in 1930 and the land was used as the site for the Cherry Orchard Estate and primary school.

Cherry Orchard Farm, *c.* 1896. Perhaps this is one of the cherry trees which gave the farm its attractive name.

Above and opposite above: Hamstead Farm, *c.* 1900.

Hamstead Mill adjoining Hamstead Farm on the River Tame, *c.* 1900. This was one of the oldest mills on the Upper Tame, being valued at 2s in the 1086 Domesday Book, when it was held by Drogo from his overlord, William Fitz Ansculf.

Left: Hamstead Mill, *c.* 1900. Frank Andrews was the miller in 1920 and was probably the last to operate the mill as a corn mill. By 1928, it was derelict and the pool was silted up. In 1951, however, it was driving a circular saw for packing-case making so it must have enjoyed a brief revival.

Below: Mill wheel at Hamstead Mill, *c.* 1900.

Hamstead Mill and dam, *c.* 1900.

Hamstead Mill, *c.* 1900. This peaceful scene shows the mill pool and cows grazing in the meadows.

The river Tame in 1897. The area still looks very rural at this time although the river Tame was already heavily polluted.

The river Tame near Hamstead Bridge in 1900.

two

Trade and Industry

A statue of James Watt. This memorial statue of the famous
engineer was executed by Sir Francis Chantrey in 1824-25 and
stands in St Mary's church in a special chapel. It was exhibited at
the Royal Academy in 1824.

Opposite above: A view of Soho Manufactory in the early nineteenth century. In 1761 Matthew
Boulton had obtained a lease of a water mill on the Hockley Brook at Soho and quickly started to
build a new factory on the site. In 1775, James Watt entered into partnership with Boulton and
Soho Manufactory became well-known and was visited by many eminent people. Handsworth can
claim to have contributed significantly to the onset of the Industrial Revolution.

Opposite below: Part of the site of the original Soho Manufactory in 1899. When this site on the
east side of South Road was excavated in September 1995, it was found to be the old location of
the Soho Mint. The Soho Manufactory ceased to operate on the death of James Watt jnr, in 1848
and was unfortunately demolished in 1863. No trace of it remains today.

THE SOHO.

A river scene near Forge Mill in 1891. On the western edge of Handsworth, a forge operated from the late sixteenth century and a furnace producing iron, probably for the nail trade, and a slitting mill were also here from a later date. In the nineteenth century, it was worked as a corn mill and this continued until the First World War.

The mill wheel at Forge Mill in 1906.

A pumping engine at Sandwell Park colliery, *c.* 1900. The old beam engine, seen in this photograph, used to pump water from the mine. It was said to be of the same type as James Watt's engines but made by another firm.

The rope walk looking towards Soho Road station in 1898. Rope was manufactured here until about 1914. The church spire in the background belongs to St Michael's church.

The site of the rope walk by Soho station in November 1981.

The Mill House in Grosvenor Road, *c.* 1970.

Drew's Flour Mill in Grosvenor Road, *c.* 1970.

A farrier at work in Handsworth in the 1920s. A farrier would shoe horses and would also act as a horse doctor.

Opposite below: The old cab proprietor's house in 1914. This was on the corner of Villa Road and Heathfield Road at Villa Cross. The site was later occupied by the Villa Cross picture house. On the left of the lower left window is a playbill advertising *Aladdin* at the Aston Hippodrome.

Right: The Soho clock factory's sale catalogue, dated 1934. This was a well-known clock-making firm in Handsworth, which was operated by W.F. Evans.

Below: The Handsworth urban district water cart. This photograph is undated but it must have been taken earlier than 1911 when Handsworth was absorbed into the city of Birmingham. Not everyone had clean drinking water in their houses at this time so water carts were necessary.

By direction of Messrs. W. F. Evans & Sons
who are retiring from business.

"The Soho Clock Factory"

154, SOHO ROAD, HANDSWORTH,

BIRMINGHAM, 21.

Catalogue

of the

HIGH—CLASS

CLOCKMAKERS' PLANT,

MACHINERY and STOCK

To be Sold by Auction without reserve

on

Thursday and Friday, September 27th & 28th, 1934.

AT 11 A.M. EACH DAY

Auctioneers

BRIGHT WILLIS & SON

F·A·I

BIRMINGHAM. — — — SOLIHULL.

BIRMINGHAM REFERENCE LIBRARY.

E.G. Wrigley & Co. Ltd, *c.* 1923. This was a firm of small tool-makers in Foundry Lane, just over the border of Handsworth in Smethwick.

The interior of E.G. Wrigley & Co. Ltd, *c.* 1923.

E.G. Wrigley & Co. Ltd, *c.* 1923. Some rear axles are being assembled in this picture.

The training school at E.G. Wrigley & Co. Ltd, *c.* 1923.

A Handsworth Dairies' milk float in the 1950s. Handsworth Dairies had premises in Island Road from the early 1900s. The White family, who operated the business, were originally farmers in Gloucestershire. Horses were used to deliver milk on some rounds until 1960. On May Day they were decorated as in this photograph – and a very colourful sight it was!

Morris' commercial cars at the Soho works in 1928. This factory was also on the fringes of Handsworth and Smethwick.

Works on the corner of Whitmore Street and Ford Street on 15 November 1961. The firm of John Rabone & Sons Ltd, rule makers, was established in 1784 and only ceased trading towards the end of the twentieth century when it was known as Rabone Chesterman.

H. Samuel's factory in Hunter's Road, *c.* 1960. In 1802, Harriet Samuel took over her father-in-law's clock-making business in Liverpool. She moved the business to Manchester where her son developed the retail jewellery business. In 1912, the business moved to Birmingham, which was the centre of the jewellery trade; a factory was subsequently built in Hunter's Road. A new factory was built in 1958 and was joined to the old one by a bridge across the road. The firm is now part of the Signet Group Plc.

Workshop at 45 Hockley Hill on 16 March 1967. The firm of W.A. Humphries Ltd, metal spinners, occupied these premises at this time.

Workshop at 45 Hockley Hill on 16 March 1967.

three

Houses

Soho House in 1906. This was the home of Matthew Boulton from 1766 until his death in 1809. Boulton made many improvements to the house which was originally built in about 1757. Most of these were carried out in the 1790s, to the designs of the architect James Wyatt. Also at this time, a park was laid out around the house and the nearby manufactory. The house had several uses after Boulton's death, including one as a girls' school. In 1990 Birmingham Museums and Art Gallery began to restore the house which opened to the public in October 1995, furnished with many items which actually belonged to Boulton.

MATTHEW BOULTON, ESQ. F.R.S. & S.A.

From an original Picture by SIR WILLIAM BEECHEY, R.A. *in the Possession of his Son, Matthew Robinson Boulton, Esq.*

Drawn by W. Evans, Engraved by A. Cardon.

An early nineteenth-century engraving of Matthew Boulton. Boulton was already an established manufacturer at Soho when he went into partnership with James Watt. Besides buttons and buckles, he made cut steel jewellery, sword hilts, Sheffield plate, sterling silverware and ormolu objects such as clocks and candelabra. Josiah Mason called Boulton the 'most complete manufacturer in metals in England'.

Opposite below: Heathfield, c. 1890. The home of James Watt until his death in 1819, Heathfield was designed by Samuel Wyatt and built between 1787 and 1790. James Watt's workshop within the house was transferred to the Science Museum in London but sadly the house itself was demolished in 1928 and the land was used for building.

Above: Prospect Hill House in 1812. This was the home of Francis Eginton, who was best known for his paintings on glass. His artistic talents were diverse and he also worked as an engraver. The views in Stebbing Shaw's *History of Staffordshire*, including this one, were engraved by him.

Left: An engraved portrait of Francis Eginton (1737–1805). While a young man, Eginton was employed by Matthew Boulton as an engraver, modeller and decorator of japanned wares. In 1781 he began to stain and paint on glass and in fact revived this largely forgotten art. His commissions in stained glass included the east window of St Paul's church in Birmingham, which depicts the conversion of St Paul.

Prospect Hill House in 1871. This photograph must have been taken just prior to the demolition of the house which stood in Soho Hill almost opposite Soho House and manufactory. In 1784, Eginton set up in business on his own account and his workshop adjoining the house can just be seen on the right of the picture. Nelson, accompanied by Sir William and Lady Hamilton, visited his showroom on 29 August 1802.

Thornhill House in 1898. Built in 1826, this house was the home of Matthew Boulton's daughter, Anne. It was on the south side of Soho Road, almost opposite the council offices and library and close to the rope walk.

Another view of Thornhill House in 1898. The name survives in nearby Thornhill Road.

Old Rosehill House. This house was near the Toll Gate at the junction of Villa Road and Soho Road. The gate posts and part of the gate can be seen in this engraving.

Church Hill House, *c.* 1950. Rebuilt about 1840, this house became the Endwood Hotel in the 1930s. The Muntz family lived there around the 1880s.

Hamstead Hall in 1897. The old hall was built in about 1450 but was destroyed, possibly by fire, before 1690 when Sir John Wyrley began to rebuild it. In 1735 it was enlarged and in this form the hall survived until 1936 when it was demolished and the land was used for building the Hamstead Hall estate. In its time, Hamstead Hall had stood in a park of about 360 acres. It was described in Nightingale's *Beauties of England and Wales,* published in 1813, as, 'the grounds of Hamstead winding along the banks of the Tame are pleasing and romantic being covered with a profusion of stately trees'.

Park Hill House, *c.* 1935. Built in about 1790, this house stood on Hamstead Hill. After having several owners, it was sold to Frederick Arthur Walton in 1890. F.A. Walton also bought Hawthorn House (see pp.52-53), hoping to develop the area for housing. This scheme was not carried out at the time and the house survived until the late 1960s.

The Friary in 1906. This house was situated in Friary Road opposite the Handsworth Theological College. It was built in 1658 as a farmhouse and was extended in about 1700. The Freer family owned it at one time; one member of the family was a founder of Birmingham's general hospital and another, the Revd Thomas Lane Freer, was the rector of Handsworth from 1803 until 1835.

The Friary on 21 June 1937. The timbering was added to the house sometime after 1906. The house was let to Frederick Arthur Walton, a manufacturing jeweller and member of the Handsworth Urban District Council. He was well-known as having the largest collection of cacti in England in his greenhouses. He died in 1922.

Hawthorn House, c. 1950. This is one of the very few Handsworth mansions to have survived. It was built in 1794 by George Birch, the Lord of the Manor. The main driveway led from Friary Road with Hawthorn Lodge at the entrance. A second drive, also with a lodge, led from Hamstead Hall Road. The last residential owner of Hawthorn House was Charles Darby who sold it in 1946 to Birmingham Corporation. Until 1981, it was a residential nursery for babies and handicapped children. Refurbishment of the building started in 1987 and, on 21 March 1988, part of it opened as a public library, the other part being occupied by the social services department.

Opposite above: Hawthorn House before its restoration started in 1987. The stable building was demolished.

Opposite below: Hawthorn House showing the inside of the stable building before demolition.

Enderley in Hawthorn Park in Friary Road in 1900. This house was built by John Haseler in 1900.

Manwoods, *c.* 1890. Built on the very edge of Handsworth by Henry Ford in about 1680, Manwoods was a farmhouse originally called Bayes Hall. In this photograph, the red–brick gabled house is almost hidden by three old yew trees which stood inside the wall. Outside the gate is a mounting block used when mounting on horseback. Manwoods was demolished in 1969.

The Leveretts in May 1907. This house, with its two lodges at the entrance, stood on the site of the Handsworth cemetery. It was built in about 1700 and demolished in 1930.

Handsworth cemetery in 1946. This photograph shows the two lodges of The Leveretts in a dilapidated condition shortly before they were demolished.

Above: No. 6 Soho Road in 19 June 1958. Once known as Rose Hill House, although apparently not the same house as in the engraving on p.49, this house was built in about 1860 and was occupied by Thomas Aston, who had run a school in the area since the 1830s. A study of the building took place in 2002 when it was already derelict.

Left: Sutton House at 91 Hall Road, *c.* 1924. With its ornate doorway and decoration beneath the eaves, this Victorian house is typical of the grander housing in parts of Handsworth. The Marsh family were living there when this picture was taken.

No. 6 Soho Road in 1909. This house is the same as the one on the facing page and shows that it had changed very little between 1909 and 1958.

Bendall's corner in November 1981. This building, in the arts and crafts style, is on the corner of Hamstead Road and Villa Road where the old toll house and gate used to be. When it was built in 1904 it was called Ye Olde Toll Gate House.

Numbers 34-42 Villa Road in January 1981. These attractive three-storey, single-bay houses set at an angle to the road were built in around 1830-1840. The two-storey house with a three-bay front is slightly later. They are all listed buildings.

Numbers 23 and 25 Villa Road in January 1981. These small, red-brick houses were also built in around 1830-1840 and are listed buildings.

Old houses on the site of Handsworth Technical School in Golds Hill Road in November 1897.

Union Row off Grove Lane in April 1970.

Left: Mr Jolly's House at 224 Wellington Road. This old house had a bakehouse at the back, with a chimney which can be seen on the left of the picture. Mr Jolly lived there until at least the 1970s.

Below: Brown's Green Lodge on 19 April 1937. This is a nineteenth-century cottage orné with a roof supported on tree trunks and branches forming ogee arches. The thatched roof has now been replaced with tiles. It was the lodge to a large house called Brown's Green. In the early nineteenth century, Brown's Green was the home of Nathaniel Gooding Clarke, who was the King's Counsel in the notorious 1818 Mary Ashford murder case. Brown's Green Lodge later became Hamstead Hill School under Mr T.C. Lowe.

Right and below: The Anchorage at 137 Handsworth Wood Road, *c.* 1900. The firm Crouch & Butler were the architects of this handsome house which was built for Mr Constantine in 1899. The furniture was designed by the architects and the copper work in the oak, copper and stone fireplace was executed by the Bromsgrove Guild, possibly by Benjamin Creswick. The murals and minstrels' gallery were unfortunately destroyed by fire in the 1970s. The house is now occupied by a Christian group.

HANDSWORTH WOOD
Cherry Orchard Estate . . The new Garden Suburb.

WELL-BUILT SEMI-DETACHED VILLAS WITH CAVITY WALLS AND EVERY MODERN CONVENIENCE.

THESE houses are in a delightful situation amidst country scenery and yet only 15 minutes from the City. Worlds End Road leads off Handsworth Wood Road, and there is a frequent 'bus service, and also a good service of trains from Handsworth Wood Station.

The builders are Messrs. Wm. Wilkinson, Ltd., of Hutton Road, Handsworth, the well-known building contractors. This firm's first-class work will justify the confidence of purchasers. The houses have a pleasant and varied elevation of brindle brick and rough-cast, with prominent dormers and well-constructed bays. The tiled roofs have a good pitch and are torched from the inside. The gable ends are built with cement mortar.

Each house has a minimum frontage of 10 yards with a total area of about 500 square yards, and ample space for a garage.

The Accommodation includes :

Pleasant square hall with Cloak Room ; Lounge, 15ft. × 12ft., including bay ; Dining Room, 15ft. × 12ft. 6in., including bay ; pleasant Kitchen, 9ft. × 10ft., with fireplace, enamelled gas boiler, deep sink, draining board, and dresser. The walls are plastered. Light Pantry. Three good-sized Bedrooms and Box Room. Tiled Bathroom with block bath and plated taps, wash-hand basin and airing cupboard. Separate Lavatory. Lounge and dining room floors stained surrounds. Outside Lavatory and Coal House.

Electric light, gas and water laid on. Electric power plugs. Aerial in roof. Copper circulation pipes. Latest design grates and mantelpieces. Purchasers have choice of wallpapers. Front garden paths concreted. Posts and chain fence.

MAIN DRAINAGE.   **Price - £525**   **NO ROAD CHARGES.**

Ground rent, £6. Leasehold for 99 years. Free legal conveyance, except stamp duty. Total rates including water about 6/6 per week.

The Birmingham Incorporated Building Society will advance a mortgage of £475 at 5%. Interest and repayments 14/7 per week.

The structure and construction of these houses is sound, and purchasers are invited to obtain expert opinion if they desire.

The houses are good value and are complete in every respect. They are well worth the attention of those who desire a comfortable labour-saving house in a healthy, convenient garden suburb.

Further particulars from :—

SYDNEY L. CLIFTON, Estate Agent.
Telephone : MIDland 4669.   47, TEMPLE ROW, BIRMINGHAM 2.

Cherry Orchard estate, *c.* 1936. Built in the 1930s on the site of Cherry Orchard Farm, this estate consists mainly of semi-detached houses. Some shops and a post office were built in Cooper's Road and a primary school was built in Cherry Orchard Road.

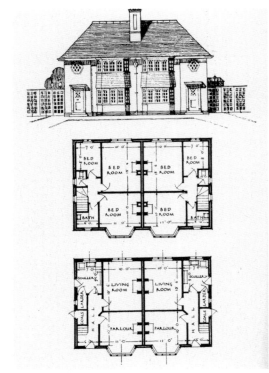

Handsworth Wood Estates Ltd in 1932. Hamstead Hall estate, on the site of the old manor house, was one of the estates developed by this company in the 1930s. This design is one of several specimen houses pictured in the firm's brochure and is typical of suburban housing of the period.

four

Churches, Public Buildings and Schools

St Mary's church, *c.* 1890. For centuries this was the only church in the large, sprawling parish of Handsworth. Although in existence by 1200, there is little remaining of its early structure. Major alterations were carried out by William Hollins in 1820 and a chapel was added by Thomas Rickman to house Chantrey's statue of James Watt in 1826. J.A. Chatwin altered the church again from 1876-80. James Watt, Matthew Boulton and William Murdock are all buried here.

St Mary's church in October 1960. This postcard view shows the attractive setting of Handsworth's parish church.

The front view of Handsworth rectory, *c.* 1890. The rectory stood approximately where the boating pool in Handsworth park now is.

St Michael's church in Soho Hill in the mid-nineteenth century. This church was built by William Bourne in 1855, and the tower and spire were added to it in 1868.

St Andrew's church in Oxhill Road, *c.* 1910. W.H. Bidlake was the architect of this church, built in red and blue brick, with stone facings, in 1907. Some interior furnishings are by other arts and crafts artists such as the processional cross by Edward Jones.

St James' church in 1918. Situated in Crocketts Road, this church was built between 1838 and 1840 on land donated by John Crockett of the New Inns. Designed originally by R. Ebbles, it was enlarged in 1895 by J.A. Chatwin.

Cannon Street Memorial church in Soho Road, *c.* 1930. Cannon Street Baptist church in Birmingham was founded in 1737. The chapel closed in 1879 and the congregation moved to Mount Zion chapel in Graham Street, and eventually moved to Cannon Street Memorial church, built in 1930.

The interior of Westminster Road's congregational church, *c.* 1890. Ingall & Hughes designed this church in the gothic style. It opened in 1879.

Hamstead Road Baptist church in January 1981. When the congregation of Mount Zion chapel in Graham Street moved to Hagley Road in 1882, a small number of members formed a new church which was erected in 1883 to the design of J.P. Osborne.

Above and below: The Bishop of Birmingham, Bishop Gore, laying the foundation stone at Handsworth cemetery on 22 September 1909.

Opposite below: Handsworth cemetery and chapel in November 1981. The Handsworth Urban District Council purchased The Leveretts estate in 1906 from the Sandwell Park Colliery Co. to lay out a new cemetery. The chapel, designed by W.H. Bidlake, was opened on 1 October 1910 by the chairman of Handsworth council, T. Henry Berry JP. In 1911, the cemetery passed into the care of Birmingham Corporation.

Handsworth Wesleyan Theological College in Friary Road, *c.* 1880. This is a large college building, formerly a theological college for training Methodist ministers. It was designed by Ball & Goddard in a Tudor style and built in 1880–81. The college is now the Hamstead campus of the University of Central England.

An aerial view of the Wesleyan College in 1926.

Above: The convent of Our Lady of Mercy in Hunter's Road during the mid-nineteenth century. These convent buildings were designed by Augustus Welby Pugin and built from 1840–41. The original chapel was unfortunately bombed in 1942 and a new chapel was built in the late 1950s.

Right: The cloister of the convent of Our Lady of Mercy in Hunter's Road, *c.* 1980. Unusually sited on steeply sloping ground, the cloister has an open timber roof and a tiled floor.

Handsworth Old Town Hall in Slack Lane in November 1981. This late fifteenth or early sixteenth century timber-framed building of three bays still survives. The photograph clearly shows the cruck-frame construction which used naturally curved timbers. The building was altered in the seventeenth century and modernised in 1946, having originally been one house. It was called the Old Town Hall because it had been used as a constable's house or court house where travelling assize courts were held. Part of the building is now used by the Handsworth Historical Society for their meetings, exhibitions and open days.

Left: Handsworth Old Town Hall in 1946. This view shows the interior after renovation, with one of the massive oak beams which support the upper floor.

Opposite below: The police station in Holyhead Road in 1938. A new police station was built next to the old one in 1938 to the design of H.J. Manzoni, the Birmingham city engineer and surveyor.

The police station in Holyhead Road on 25 January 1937. The overhead cables for trams are visible in this photograph.

The Rhodes alms houses in Soho Road, *c.* 1890. Sir Benjamin Stone took this photograph of the Rhodes alms houses, which were erected in memory of John Rhodes of Waverhill in Handsworth by his wife in 1871.

Grove Lane baths, *c.* 1980. The public baths in Grove Lane were opened on 28 January 1907 to the design of J.P. Osborne. They consisted of two swimming baths, private baths and Turkish baths. The water was obtained from a 500ft well sunk especially for the purpose. Unhappily these fine baths, which were popular with local residents and used by local schools, have now been closed.

The Handsworth library and council offices on 22 September 1982. These were the offices of the local board of Handsworth and later Handsworth Urban District Council until 1911 when Handsworth became part of Birmingham. They were built by Alexander and Henman in 1878–79. Handsworth library occupies the left-hand side of the building, while the rest is used by the city council as offices.

The interior of Handsworth library on 22 September 1982. This library is held in great affection by local people. Countless children must have been introduced to the joys of reading in its wonderful children's room while older residents might remember the days when a closed access system operated here.

Birmingham Municipal Bank and the showrooms of Birmingham's electric supply department in the 1930s. On the corner of Clarence Road and Holyhead Road, this typical 1930s building was designed by the architects Collier & Keyte.

The infant welfare institute, Hunter's Road, in the 1930s. The Carnegie Institute in Hunter's Road was a gift to the city from the Carnegie trustees and was opened in October 1923. Andrew Carnegie was a Scotsman who emigrated to the United States and amassed a fortune which he spent mainly on building public libraries. On his death, the Carnegie Trust was formed and grants were made for other purposes such as child welfare work; infant welfare institutes were given to four major cities, of which Birmingham was one.

Above and below: Handsworth Technical School in Golds Hill Road from the academic year 1912–13 (above) and 1913–14 (below). The photograph below is from the school's prospectus and shows the advanced mechanical laboratory.

Handsworth Grammar School in Grove Lane in 1907. Handsworth Grammar School was opened in 1862 by the Handsworth Bridge Trust and was once known as Bridge Trust School. In 1906 it became a pupil-teacher centre and this photograph shows a group of pupil-teachers taken in 1907. The pupil-teacher scheme was a method of training teachers by a combination of practical experience in the classroom and evening classes.

Handsworth Grammar School in the academic year 1906-07. This photograph shows pupils at work in the classroom. Using guesswork, it seems likely that they were using hand-mirrors to make sure their sounds were being produced correctly, either in elocution lessons or perhaps in French lessons.

King Edward VI Grammar School for Girls in Rose Hill Road in 1911. This school was built in 1911 and was formed by amalgamating three King Edward's schools: the girls' school at Aston which had opened in 1883, and the schools in Summer Hill and Bath Row. The King Edward VI Foundation originated in 1553 but was only for the education of boys until 1883.

King Edward VI Grammar School for Girls in Rose Hill Road in 1911. The building must have been advanced for its time as it was well-equipped with a gymnasium, cookery and art rooms, a lecture theatre, science laboratories and even a playroom in which to spend wet lunch and play times. The assembly hall is particularly attractive and in the 1950s still had the same elegant light fittings.

Left: Handsworth New Road School, *c.* 1980. This attractive school building was designed by H. Buckland and E. Haywood-Farmer, who won a competition for its design. It was built in 1901.

Below: Handsworth church school, *c.* 1907. This was St Mary's Church of England Primary School, originally Handsworth National School, founded in 1812-13.

Handsworth Wood School in 1920. At this period, this private school was at Field House, 101 Church Lane and the head teacher was Clement Gibbs Mould. It moved to 17 Wellington Road and in the 1950s was known locally as 'Mr Foot's', the head teacher being G.K.F. Foot.

A hansom cab outside The Laurels School, *c.* 1900. This private school stood at the corner of Handsworth Wood Road and Wood Lane. For many years it was run by Miss Kathleen Lowe, the daughter of T.C. Lowe of Hamstead Hill School. The school continued under Mrs Rowley until 1961 when it closed; the house was subsequently sold and demolished.

Handsworth Woods Boys' School in Church Lane, *c*. 1960. The school opened in 1958 as a county modern school and later became a comprehensive. In 1998 it closed after problems caused falling numbers and the building was taken over by Handsworth Wood Girls' School.

Cherry Orchard Primary School, *c*. 1952. Opened in 1947 to serve the Cherry Orchard housing estate, the school was reorganised in 1948 by amalgamating it with Wood Lane Temporary County Primary School. This was housed in a wooden pavilion on Handsworth Wood's playing fields and was subsequently used as an annexe to the school. The first headmistress of the school was Miss Maisie Lyster.

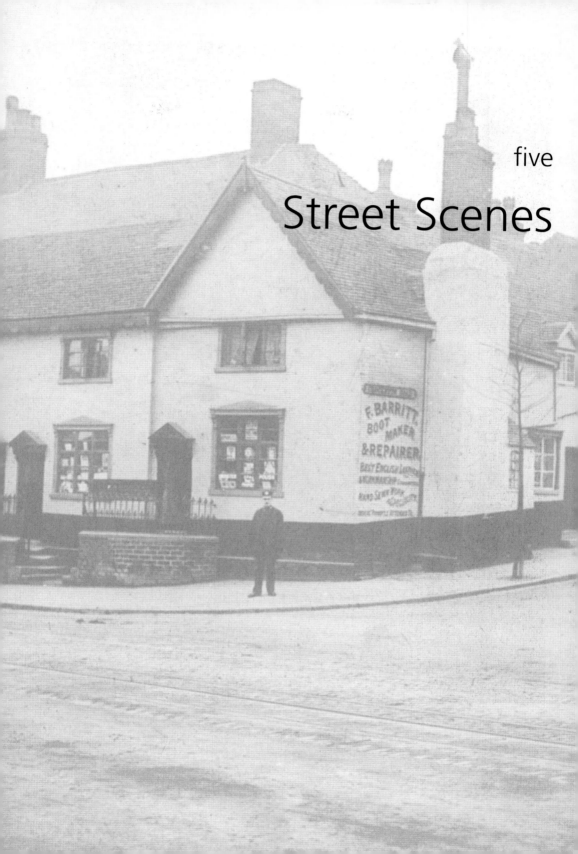

five

Street Scenes

A general view of Soho Road on 6 June 1958. The clock on the Handsworth library and council house can be seen on the right. This is one of the shopping areas of Handsworth with its collection of small shops.

Opposite above: Cable tram on Soho Road in 1900. Cable trams took over from the standard gauge horse tramway on this route after 1886. They were eventually replaced by electric trams. Soho Road is one of the main thoroughfares in Handsworth.

Opposite below: A handsome row of shops in Soho Road in 1958.

Soho Road looking towards Birmingham, *c.* 1980.

Soho Road in February 1985. Since the 1950s, the Soho Road area of Handsworth has seen immigration from the West Indies and the Indian sub-continent. The shops and people in the street reflect this ethnic diversity.

A milestone near the corner of Milestone Lane on 29 June 1971. The milestone is thought to date from about 1800 or a little earlier. The distances given are 111 miles from London, 3 miles from Birmingham and 10 miles from Wolverhampton.

No.9 Langdale Croft on 13 June 1955. The house on the left is typical of suburban housing built between the First and Second World Wars while the terraced houses in the background are considerably older.

Soho Road looking towards West Bromwich in February 1985.

The junction of Soho Road and Queen's Head Road, *c.* 1980. The Queen's Head public house is partially visible on the right of the picture.

Soho Hill in November 1981. This photograph shows the approximate site of the Shell Pool, a small pool in the grounds of Soho House which was drained in 1898.

Whitehall Road, c. 1920. This is a typical residential road leading off Soho Road.

Cottages on the corner of Holyhead Road and Crocketts Road, *c.* 1890.

The same Holyhead and Crocketts Road cottages photographed this time on 17 March 1937. Very little has changed in this scene although the cottages are no longer whitewashed.

Above and below: Claremont Road on 14 February 1963.

Oxhill Road on 5 June 1956. Oxhill Road was another important road in Handsworth as there was a good selection of shops there.

Oxhill Road on 5 June 1956. At the end of Oxhill Road, Handsworth opens out and looks over the cemetery and golf course, giving a feeling of its more rural past.

The junction of Grove Lane and Arthur Road on 5 May 1976.

Grove Lane on 5 May 1976.

A bomb scare near Boulton Road in October 1974. This occurred at the height of the IRA bombing campaign on mainland Britain and only one month before the Birmingham pub bombings so every warning was being taken seriously.

Sandwell Road from Oxhill Road in November 1981.

Richmond Road on 14 February 1963. A recent snowfall has turned to slush in this photograph, providing hazardous conditions for pedestrians and motorists alike. This was one of the most severe winters of the twentieth century.

Wellington Road on 2 February 1955. Gray's motor car dealers is shown on this photograph on the corner of Wellington Road and Grosvenor Road where Drew's flour mill can just be seen. The ring road sign refers to the outer circle bus route which runs for 25 miles around Birmingham.

A bus crash in Hamstead Road on
20 August 1960 had occurred just
opposite the Baptist church, and the
damaged shop front and lamp standard
obviously attracted the attention of some
local schoolboys when this photograph
was taken.

Hamstead Road in January 1981. This butcher and slaughterhouse had been close to the junction
with Villa Road for many years. It is now a Halal butcher for the large local Asian population.

Heathfield Road in November 1981. This view is taken from Mayfield Road. The name comes from the former Heathfield Estate which was the home of James Watt.

The junction of Factory Road and Piers Road in November 1981. This is in the area of Handsworth known as Gib Heath.

Westminster Road on 1 February 1963. This is another picture taken during the severe winter of 1963 as the piles of grimy snow illustrate.

Looking west in Church Lane on 1 March 1926. Although only slightly further out in Handsworth Wood, Church Lane had large houses and gardens which gave it a more leafy appearance.

Above: Church Lane on 3 May 1926. The horse-drawn cart in the distance may have been delivering bread to this rather affluent neighbourhood.

Right: No. 177 Church Lane on 10 April 1962. This large house would have been built between the First and Second World Wars.

Handsworth Wood Road on 16 February 1961. Handsworth Wood Road and beyond was developed with large, rather opulent houses throughout the nineteenth and early twentieth centuries. Manufacturers from Birmingham's jewellery quarter and also from West Bromwich and other nearby industrial areas lived here.

Handsworth Wood Road on 27 March 1973. The houses here are all individually designed for wealthy businessmen.

College Road on 7 December 1970. Handsworth's Theological College is in the grounds behind the fence on the left of the picture while Handsworth Old Town Hall can be glimpsed in the background.

Friary Road in November 1981. This is the site of one of the Friary's old lodges.

A horse-drawn carriage in Selborne Road, *c.* 1903. This very grand carriage with its team of four horses must have been here for some important occasion but this has long since been forgotten.

Hollycroft Road in the 1930s. These are parlour-type houses with slated roofs on the Farcroft estate between Rookery Road and Sandwell Road.

Oxhill Road in September 1980.

The corner of Church Lane and Hamstead Road from Wellington Road in November 1981. On the right of the picture is a block of flats where a large house called Endwood Court once stood. The lodge is still standing just round the corner in Handsworth Wood Road.

Soho Hill from Hockley Flyover on 16 March 1967.

Hockley Flyover, *c.* 1970. Soho Hill rises steeply on the left of the photograph beneath the flyover. The white-painted bingo hall on the left beyond the flyover was once the New Palladium cinema, which closed in 1962.

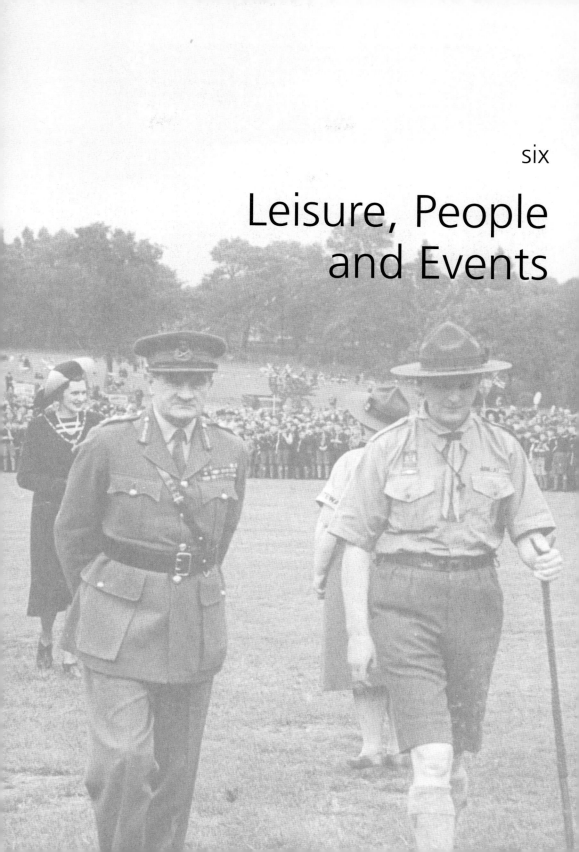

six

Leisure, People and Events

The extension to Victoria Park near the site of the old rectory in 1895. One of the glories of Handsworth is its magnificent park, originally known as Victoria Park to commemorate the golden jubilee of Queen Victoria in 1887, but now called simply Handsworth Park. Originally part of The Grove estate, some of it, including the house called The Grove, was purchased and opened as a park in 1888. Additions to the original 20 acres were made in 1890 and 1895, and the size of the park eventually became 63 acres.

A view of the land added to Handsworth Park in 1895. This was on the Grove Lane side of the park near to Grove Farm.

A postcard view of Handsworth Park showing the boating lake and boathouse, *c.* 1920.

The Grove house in Handsworth Park in 1913. This postcard view indicated that it was the park ranger's house at this time. Later it housed refreshment rooms but in 1968 it was demolished.

The procession of motor cars at the Thornhill Road gates of Handsworth Park on 7 July 1906. The occasion was Joseph Chamberlain's seventieth birthday celebrations.

Opposite above: The arrival of Joseph Chamberlain at Handsworth Park on 7 July 1906. The master of ceremonies was Mr J. Farnold, while the gentleman in the straw boater is Mr Brace.

Opposite below: The bandstand in Handsworth Park in 1920.

The main entrance to Handsworth Park in Hamstead Road, *c.* 1920. The girl and boy on the path are both holding hoops, which were very popular children's toys at this time.

The memorial gates at Handsworth Park, around the 1950s.

Handsworth Park Lodge, *c.* 1900. This handsome lodge stands at the Hamstead Road entrance to the park.

The new extension to the Sons of Rest pavilion in Handsworth Park, 14 March 1957. The Sons of Rest began in 1927 with a group of retired gentlemen who used to meet in one of the shelters in the park. The first pavilion was erected in 1930; a new, larger one was opened in 1937 and extended in 1957.

The thirty-fifth annual Scouts' rally on 3 July 1948. The Scouts' rally was one of the annual events which local people really looked forward to. On this occasion, Field Marshal Sir William Slim took the salute.

Opposite above: A display of gymnastics in the park in the early 1900s.

Opposite below: The sunken garden in Handsworth Park in 1933.

The floral island in Handsworth Park in 1949.

Handsworth Park on 25 January 1955. Improvement works to the boating pool are being carried out by direct labour in this photograph. The direct labour building department was set up by the city council in 1954 mainly for house-building purposes but work was also carried out for other council departments.

A snowy scene in Handsworth park on 1 December 1952.

The Birmingham Show on 31 August 1956. The city police are performing a musical ride in this photograph. The Birmingham Show, usually known as the Flower Show, was another eagerly anticipated event in Handsworth Park. It was held there until 1969 when it moved to Perry Park.

The Birmingham Show in 1956. This photograph shows the dog show in full swing. The show covered many subjects besides flowers, such as dogs, cats, rabbits, bees and honey and arena events such as horse-jumping and displays. There was also a fairground to make it an ideal day out for families with children.

Opposite above: The Birmingham Show on 4 September 1958. These boys are awaiting the opening of the show. The boy on the left is Compton Edwards and the one on the right is John Oakes.

Opposite below: Handsworth Park on 28 May 1972. These children are enjoying themselves in the children's playground in the park.

Tug of war in Handsworth Park on 19 June 1971. This was the National Tug of War Championships. The winners were to represent England at the European Championships in Sweden in September 1971 and at an international competition in Switzerland in October.

Opposite above: The boathouse in Handsworth Park in the 1960s.

Opposite below: Cyclo-cross racing in Handsworth Park on 18 April 1970.

Above and below: Booth Street's adventure playground in August 1974.

Above and below: Allotments at the Uplands in the 1950s. Allotments or leisure gardens have been a traditional feature of life in the Birmingham area, although their survival was sometimes in doubt because of a shortage of building land. In recent years, however, there has been a revival of interest in the allotments, as they enable people to acquire vegetable plots at reasonable rents. The result is home-grown vegetables and healthy exercise for the gardener!

The Red Lion Inn in Holyhead Road, opposite Boulton Road, *c.* 1900. This photograph shows the old coaching inn where stage coaches stopped for rest and refreshment and to change horses. The present Red Lion was rebuilt on the same site.

Ye Olde Barley Mow in the early 1900s. The exact position of this old inn is not known. The publican is said to be J. Burton and it is known from trade directories that he was a beer retailer at 204 Wattville Road in the late nineteenth century, so this may have been the one.

The Uplands Tavern in Oxhill Road in March 1933. The architects of this large, modern pub were Harrison & Cox.

Lemprière's balloon at Dudley Castle in the early twentieth century. To judge by the crowd in attendance, Lt Lemprière's balloon demonstrations were great crowd-pullers.

Opposite above: Villa Cross picture house in Heathfield Road on 28 December 1962. One of several cinemas in Handsworth, the Villa Cross opened in 1915 as the New Picture House. After showing Asian films from 1970 and then becoming a bingo hall, it closed in 1984 and was demolished. The van on the left of the picture belonged to a very well-known grocer's shop in Villa Road called Cross's Stores.

Opposite below: The officials of Handsworth Urban District Council in 1907. The football eleven are from left to right, back row: N.F. Spenser. Middle row: M. Jackson, J. Draper, H.W. Barker, J. Parr, N.G. Tomey, W.H. Thompson, P. Adams and H. Holmes. Front row: Simcox and Matthewman. The occasion is not known.

Left: South Staffordshire Volunteers, *c.* 1900. This shows the old drum major's scarf and staff. The volunteers existed from 1859 until 1907 when they were reorganised under the Territorial and Reserve Forces Act of that year.

Below: Handsworth volunteers who went out to the South African War, copied from the original in 1907.

Opposite above: Soho station during the First World War. 2/1st Southern General Hospital MAC cars are seen here waiting to take the wounded soldiers to the nearby hospital.

Opposite below: Handsworth Wood station in the early 1900s. This station was on the Soho, Handsworth and Perry Barr loop line which opened in 1886. Handsworth Wood station opened in 1896 and closed in 1941. It was sited in Hamstead Road opposite the Endwood public house.

Other Birmingham titles published by Tempus

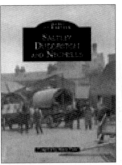

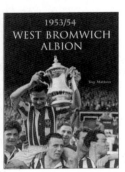

If you are interested in purchasing other books published by Tempus, or in case you have difficulty finding any Tempus books in your local bookshop, you can also place orders directly through our website

www.tempus-publishing.com